Dedication

I dedicate this book to those individuals who perceive and think, in order that they may continue to observe and share their conclusions with others. Only the individual who observes in detail will reach exact conclusions when he has an un-cluttered mind.

It was always the ideas that determined the advancement and welfare of the human being, never raw violence or war.

Acknowledgements

I wish to thank

My sister,
Dr. Diana Pengitore, ND, editor, and American Translator Association (ATA) member for her expert translation from German to English.

My brother-in-law,
Dr. Frank Pengitore, Ed.D., for his editorial expertise.

Wolfgang Fries

My Philosophy

Imprint

Copyrights and clearances

For this publication, literature from L. Ron Hubbard (LRH)[1] was utilized. The main book, *To Endure Life - The Bible of the 21st Century*, has been re-issued as *Philosophy of Life - The Book of Basics*, from which a part of this book's written texts was taken. All material contained in this book has been approved by the authors whose work has been referenced herein.

Book design and typeset:

Wolfgang Fries
Contact: Friesway@online.de

Translator and Editor: Dr. Diana Pengitore, ND
Proofreading Editor: Dr. Frank Pengitore, Ed.D.

Production and publishing:

BoD - Books on Demand
In de Tarpen 42
22848 Norderstedt; Deutschland

ISBN: 978-3-7528-9234-5
Handbook, softcover; 1. Edition

© 2018 for the content Wolfgang Fries
© 2018 Books on Demand GmbH, Norderstedt

Bibliografische Information der Deutschen Nationalbibliothek
Die Deutsche Nationalbibliothek verzeichnet diese Publikation in der Deutschen Nationalbibliografie; detaillierte bibliografische Daten sind im Internet über http://dnb.d-nb.de abrufbar. (The book is listed in the German Nationalbibliografie; detailed information is available at: http://dnb.d-nb.de)

[1]**L. Ron Hubbard**: presents in Dianetics and Scientology an explanation of the construction of the human mind and the action of the mind on matter that comprises the entire catalogue of psychosomatic illnesses, which are more than 80% of the known illnesses. In Scientology, techniques are described with which to exteriorize a person. meaning that the person is knowingly separated, with full perceptions, from the body. I am not writing in the subjunctive (possibility form) that science is used to, as they are never sure! Separating the person from his body is sure.

Important note to the reader:
Take great care in reading this text in order not to skip words that you do not understand. If you do not understand a sentence or text, it is because there is a word or words that you did not understand, or for which you have a false definition. Certain words are explained by foot notes; however, they are just the definitions of the words as they are used in the corresponding sentence. Words often have many definitions and to reach a complete understanding of a word, it is recommended that you consult a good dictionary.

My Philosophy is the first book **in a five-part series** from the book *Philosophy of Life - The Book of Basics*. This complete series is available in German. The remaining four books (*Learning how to Learn, Learning How to Understand; A Happy Relationship; To Endure Life - The Bible of the 21st Century;* and, *Past Life Regression - Introduction and Brief Guide*) will be published in English in the future. The book, *Human Rights and Obligations - Revised,* is another excellent publication recommended for inclusion in the series.

My Philosophy
(Preface to the study)

Of what use is the language, when one cannot understand the word!

Humankind

Humankind experiences the world through the mind. If the mind of humankind does not achieve order, then this world cannot get in order.

1. Humankind is a product of its actions.
2. It does what it thinks. If it thinks not to do it, it does not do it.
3. Humankind tries not to do wrong.
4. There are strange actions; henceforth, there are strange thoughts[1].
5. Humankind tries not to do wrong, but does it anyway, because thoughts exist that appear stronger than free will.
6. Therefore, thought governs humankind.
7. Therefore, it is not always the cause of its thoughts.
8. Therefore, there is a part of humanity that tells it to do wrong.
9. This part confuses it, making it small, weak and sick.
10. Being sick means to do wrong – this is what the thought instructs. Millions of years of engineering work resulted in an organism that can heal itself, and yet it gets sick.
11. Therefore, the thought organizes matter.
12. The thought is the thought of the entity.
13. All thoughts are made of the same substance, whether they are good or bad.
14. The bad thought can be eliminated. It comes from the bad experiences that the person previously accumulated - first he caused it, then he got the effect of it. (What goes around, comes around.)
15. Therefore, humankind again will get big, strong and healthy.
16. Therefore, humankind must no longer be human.

Corollary[2]: Humanity will change when it changes its thoughts. One can change humanity, when one helps to change its thoughts.

---

[1]**Thought:** (a) A memory recording as a copy of the physical universe with all perceptions.
(b) Thinking means that one creates new memory records or parts of it. One cannot think about something[3] when one has no record of it.
[2]**Corollary**: a deduction from a proposition already true.
[3]**Something**: matter, emotion, thought.

The entity

Neither medicine nor food will set one free from a problem. Only the human mind is able to solve the problem of the human mind! (LRH)

1. The entity is not the human being.
2. The entity is the person himself, who is aware of himself.
3. The entity creates energy and transforms this energy into images that are known as thoughts.
4. The accumulation of these images is known as the mind.
5. Intelligence is the utilization of energy. We take images out of the mind and arrange them into new images; therefore, we can solve perceived problems.
6. Strange thoughts hinder intelligence.
7. The entity does not lose intelligence but reduces it.
8. Death is a means by which we rid ourselves of the useless body that it has become.
9. The entity does not disappear. It supplies the new body with energy that it requires for development, being able to send it through the nerve channels, and the muscles resulting in movement.
10. The entity takes the mind along but "forgets" about it.
11. Knowledge does not get lost.
12. The entity has all capabilities, though these are blocked by thoughts!

In honor of my master, who made me realize that I am and will be.

Survival – The way of humankind

In this world, there are the "educated, the "blind" and the "sighted."
The sighted see things as they are.
The "blind" think what they should see.
The "educated" look back at the education that they received, neither looking nor thinking for themselves.

Therefore, life among the "blind" is degraded to a discipline of thinking, since it is lived in such a way as they think – except for the worker, who is below the level of the "blind" and functions just like a machine.

What is left for humankind, since it knows nothing about life and cannot see it? Even the sighted cannot see it, because life cannot be seen, although the sighted knows what it is and for this reason does not have to dream about it.

1. Survival means to support oneself.
2. To live, it is necessary to acquire the things needed for living, e.g. food, clothes, money, etc.
3. One must be able to produce a product, something that can be exchanged. Even a teacher has a product: an educated student who can take on life.
4. An idea is required prior to producing a product: The more precise the idea, the more precise the product, or the more specific the idea; the more specific the product.
5. An idea contains information. This information can be learned or acquired.
6. One becomes more competitive and increases the potential for survival by constantly improving oneself.
7. The more one can do, the higher the potential of survival.

In fact, three components for the best survival are necessary: **education, intelligence and reason**. Intelligence and education allow the development of an all-destructive weapon – meaning non-survival – and only reason prevents its action!

And above all only one thing is left: intention. Without intention nothing happens!

Getting along

How do we socialize with someone? There are traditions and customs, hence, a certain behavior that consists of certain rules – these can be in writing or not. In fact, these are the moral rules that should provide orientation about right and wrong.

A short note in passing, the Germans have a sophisticated clause in § 1 of their traffic rules and regulations. Indeed, there is social traffic to which these can be applied, as well.

(1) Participation in society requires constant attention and mutual regard.

(2) Every citizen must behave in such a way so that no one gets injured, endangered, or, depending on the circumstances, inevitably hindered or harassed.

We must remember to treat our fellow Man[1] as a friend, as he is not yet an enemy!

In peace time:

Meet all human beings with a friendly disposition and friendly intentions.
Recognize if their actions are helpful or a burden.

If their intentions are good, help them to recognize their mistakes for a better time to come.

Once the real mistake is found, and the goal still cannot be achieved, give them a task that they can do.

If they are unable to fulfill any task, we should let them go, so that they will not bring us bad luck.

A common intention lets individuals build groups, and each group has one leader. This leader should have superior intellectual qualities above all others, and, through reason, be able to lead the group to a common goal in the best way possible.

If the leader's reason fails, then the leader fails, as well as the group. From this, all can learn, especially the leader.

All group members have the right to appeal the leader's reason.

---

[1]**Man**: mankind, humans, human beings, people, persons, beings, individuals, creatures.

Love

It is not the person but rather the emotion. One assumes that if a person is lost, the emotion is lost. However, this emotion can always be created anew, because there is as much love as there are people.

1. An emotion desired by everyone.
2. Nobody knows where it comes from.
3. It can give Man great happiness or great suffering.
4. The emotion does not originate from the being itself, but from that which makes him into a human being.
5. If Man would recognize what he is made of, he could recognize himself and walk the way of life with love, which would bring him great happiness.
6. The emotion is a thought and it says: "Be together!"
7. It is one's own doing that destroys the emotion.
8. To part means to save another person from one's own bad actions because the person no longer wants to hurt another.
9. A relationship is a decision.
10. This decision is to be for someone. Note: A person can be for or against someone.
11. The decision is carried out by taking action. If one stops taking action, the decision fades.
12. Jealousy is supported by fear to decide differently. It may also indicate what the other person is thinking of doing.
13. The weak tend to be jealous.
14. The decision of the strong will persist. It is carried by reason.
15. Reason is the survival of the person in the direction of pleasure.
16. Pain means to succumb and, in the long run, not to survive.
17. Communication is the glue in a relationship; secrets lead to separation.

To fall in love is quite easy, but it requires understanding to maintain that love. If there is no mutual understanding, love falls apart. It is the messed-up mind of humanity that ends understanding.

Happiness

Life supplies a person with a happy emotion when that person helps life to live. Ask a woman how she feels after giving birth, or how someone feels after building a house, or how people react when things get repaired to their satisfaction. All of this adds to the fact that life can live.

1. It is humanity's highest goal.
2. To be happy, humanity sacrifices freedom because being happy means to have what one desires, but "to have" ends the state of freedom.
3. Thus, humanity became a victim of matter and emotion and created its own prison.
4. Matter and emotion can invert[1] and humanity will only be happy when it no longer has matter and emotion.
5. Thus, it can be concluded that when happiness is connected with matter and emotion, happiness fades, as well.
6. However, there is another form of happiness.
7. Through matter and emotion, humanity is in an effect position, as matter or emotion affects it.
8. Humanity can be a cause - responsible for how things develop!
9. When humanity has a task that fulfills it, it beautifies the world or cultivates[2] the virtue of humanity, generally improving its existence, or it allows that care is taken for things to work and are of use, or that bring joy to humanity. With those actions, humanity will experience satisfaction and happiness.
10. Thus, we conclude that humanity creates its own luck by doing.
11. Even the person, who still has a bit of hope to succeed in something, carries a bit of luck within. As hope dissipates, the person completely gives up and, therefore, has given up on luck.
12. Humanity will fall ill if suppression or counter-intentions have become too big for it to reach its happiness, and it will depart from life – in ways that may be obvious or concealed – only to escape misfortune.
13. Humanity can be happy if it is strong and recognizes the fundamentals of symbiosis[3] and reason and abides by them; therefore, there can be happiness for everyone.

---

[1] **Invert**: to reverse in position, order, or relationship (from good to bad, from functional to broken, etc.)
[2] **Cultivate**: to improve by labor, care, or study.
[3] **Symbiosis**: a relationship of mutual benefit or dependence.

The inability to understand, ignorance, indiscipline, clumsiness and cowardice are the main factors that stand in the way of happiness.

Happiness means to set something in motion, either toward or away from someone. Humanity wants to have or to get rid of things!

How can it achieve this when it is defeated by one of the properties mentioned above?

Work

1. Work is there to be done.
2. When it gets done, humanity prospers.
3. To recognize the work and to do it will ensure the survival of humanity
4. Things of complexity should be divided, so that they become transparent and predictable.
5. Finish one thing after the other.
6. Develop a strategy before every action. Minutes of reflection can save hours of work.
7. Stay up-to-date.
8. Every mistake is the door for an attack.
9. Professionalism means to be perfect.
10. Work is enjoyable when it is really understood.
11. Give energy[1] from where it comes – mistreatment of employees or low wages will result in not having any more employees.
12. Work methods and experiences should be recorded, so they remain.
13. "You reap what you sow."

To perceive the work

It starts with people recognizing what is in front of them. They see it, and ask themselves: "Does this belong there?" and "Is it in the right condition/order?" Well, fix it, or put it away, whatever the case may be.

This also applies, to anything that goes wrong, whether at home, at work, or in any social matter. To perceive the work also means to notice a deficiency: Something is missing that can optimize a procedure and can help people to continue in a situation.

To be or not to be?

Each time people decide not to do the work, it is a step in the direction of "not to be." See what will happen in the long run when the work does not get done!

---

[1]**Energy**: makes things move; energy is needed to survive; consider symbiosis.

Understanding

1. Humankind uses words or symbols to convey information.
2. This information is about a concept and not about the word. The purpose of the word should be to understand the concept.
3. Every word contains a concept. Assembling words into a sentence results in a larger or more precise concept. Assembling sentences into books results in a general concept.
4. A general concept consists of things, persons and intentions. With a general concept, people expound about what happens to things.
5. Understanding, by means of the concept, is expressed with the word, as words are only a substitute for concepts.
6. Humankind will not understand if it only has letters or symbols with which to work. It will only understand when it has a visual image of the transferred concept. Therefore, it can understand through direct observation. Words and symbols have leeway, direct observations do not.
7. Beginning to recognize the purpose and the intent of a general concept is the basis of understanding.
8. Strength, free will and logic are the main points of understanding a physical universe.
9. Understanding is superior to things. People must decide whether they support or neglect them.
10. Humankind then can distinguish right from wrong, only when it understands.
11. Humankind will have a better chance for survival, only when it can differentiate right from wrong, as the sum of the right decisions determines its existence.

People are superior to the things that they understand. With a complete lack of understanding, they are no longer able to initiate the appropriate actions.

When people try to understand, they ask for logic – another word for logic is logical consistency. They do this by trying to recognize a sequential concatenation[1] of events. Therefore, the individual things of the universe have their logic, be it physics with its correlation of force and matter, mathematics and languages with their rules, human laws, mechanics with levers, shafts and cogwheels, electronics with capacitors, shunts, resistors, and electrical energy, or music with harmonic sounds, etc. and, of course, people with their free will and oddities.

[1]**Concatenation**: to link together in a series or chain.

People often may not seem logical with their actions, but they act based on their free will, ideas and convictions.

When they do not know the will, ideas and convictions of the acting person, they will not recognize a logical consistency. Regarding humankind, logic works in two directions: good or bad, or right or wrong, depending how it is perceived. It is a personal point of view.

Awareness

People can know about something when they are familiar with it.

1. People are aware of something when they know about it. Awareness increases with knowledge.
2. Knowledge is information.
3. Information is obtained from oneself or others by reading books or from personal experiences.
4. Information is valuable as it is:
   - Understood,
   - Applied,
   - Brings about a result.
5. An opinion is a personal evaluation of data[1].
6. An opinion does not change things as they are, but it can change their value.
7. The value of a matter determines its promotion.
8. Things will be of value when they fulfill the definition of symbiosis.
9. Symbiosis is co-existing for a mutual use.
10. Morality is the opinion of Man.
11. Morality changes as time goes on.
12. Morality's influence often leads to a wrong evaluation of data and; therefore, it results in the corresponding behavior.
13. Ethics is the teaching about survival – right and wrong.
14. The fundamentals of ethics are always the same.
15. Currently ethics are poorly understood by people; therefore, people are mostly moral rather than ethical. They make more mistakes, as they are not very sensible.

[1]**Data**: facts or figures to be processed; evidence, records, statistics, etc. from which conclusions can be inferred; information.

The ability to observe

1. Observing is not just looking.
2. Observing means to perceive things and to recognize differences.
3. The recognized differences are used to evaluate data.
4. New data is evaluated by comparing it with familiar data.
5. People tend to think, rather than to observe.
6. Observing means to see exactly what is present, not what is being thought about it, or how it came to be.
7. Proper observing leads to logical thinking.
8. Orient on what is present and disregard any thoughts about it, including the thoughts of others.
9. Observing is the source of knowledge!

Learn to observe and to conclude logically, rather than just to think!

Truth

The truth tells us what happened. The future is uncertain and starts in the present.

1. The truth is as it is.
2. It includes place, time, form and event.
3. Strong people are capable of the truth because they can take responsibility.
4. Truth and wisdom are sown sparingly and not often encountered. Truth and knowledge are weakened when an individual seeks an unfair advantage over another.
5. *What is true for you is true.* (LRH)

Even the lie will enlighten, but only if it is recognized as such when compared with the truth – thus, the lie will strengthen the truth, letting one know with whom one is dealing.

Freedom

Freedom means to be free of something; it means not to have it.

Freedom of choice and self-determination? Freedom does not mean people can do all they want to do. It is against the basic laws of the community, and this would be anti-social.

Individuals will only be attacked by what they resist. When they give all by their own free will, and agree with everything, what could happen to them? They will lose everything and NOTHING[1] will be left, only freedom!

The cycle of nature

Microorganisms organize themselves into complex organisms to allow life to conquer the material universe. Smaller organisms are vital for the survival of larger organisms. Fungi, microorganisms and bacteria convert organic matter into humus, so plants can grow.

Plants are a food source for animals, and plants and animals are the food for people. Due to their intellectual ability, people recognize life and should serve life.

Life itself cannot pass away, even when the organism continuously undergoes the cycle of creation, survival and decay.

The game of the universe

It is the lie that keeps things in existence because the truth was the solution of the riddle; and therefore, the mission was forgotten!

Things should be; that is important!

What happens to things when people change their mind? Were they ever that important? When it is agreed to play a game, importance is assigned to things, otherwise, the game would fall apart.

---

[1]**Nothing**: (a) An indeterminate potential for creation and movement. (b) The person himself, not the body or the mind. The awareness of awareness unit (*Scientology Technical Dictionary*). It is not matter and cannot die. It has no space, no time, no wavelength, and no energy, but it can create energy.

From God to Man

1. At the beginning the NOTHING created the SOMETHING.
2. With the SOMETHING, time began.
3. The NOTHING breathed life into the SOMETHING, and there was Man.
4. The NOTHING is exactly what it is: NOTHING, but it can create everything.
5. Just as the NOTHING can create everything from nothing, so it again can make everything back into nothing; therefore, the end can be the beginning.
6. Therefore, there is no value, neither good or bad, nor right or wrong.
7. However, Man gives things value because he thinks that he is SOMETHING, and yet he is only a part of the NOTHING.
8. Man set barriers on his past that he describes as oblivion.
9. The barriers are protected by pain because Man tries to avoid pain that he is unable to confront.
10. Pain was caused first before Man could experience it.
11. Then, the pain was assigned to another source, and the entire game got out of control.
12. Man then arrived exactly where he is now!
13. Therefore, when Man confronts and eliminates the pain and deals with his past, he himself can be the beginning.
14. Then, the NOTHING can be put together with all its parts into a whole.

Note: Why this formulation of NOTHING and SOMETHING? Man is always searching for a SOMETHING, i.e. matter that is supposed to serve as scientific proof. He never searches for the NOTHING, and that is why he will never find it – whereas the NOTHING moves the SOMETHING!

Corollary:
First there was force then matter, as force forms, and assembles matter.

To walk the path

1. The pages I have written are few; however, there are the hundred thousand that let one recognize the truth.
2. People will be accompanied by others on the way.
3. People are seized by utter stupidity. Rather than to experience and to measure, they start to think, giving more importance to their own thoughts and to the words of others, as to what is going on.
4. The path requires dedication and perseverance.
5. Currently, people cannot comprehend the goal at the end, for it is so grand.
6. The **goal** is **infinity**.

Something to think about

The human being is always looking to solve the mystery of life. The Bible gives some good hints in this regard. Here are some quotations from the Gospel of John in the "Holy Book" (KJV[1]).

- 1:1-3: "The Word became flesh. In the beginning was the Word and the Word was with God and God was the Word. All things are made through the same, and without the same nothing is made, that is made."
- 13:16: "The servant is not greater than his lord; neither he that is sent greater than he that sent him."
- 6:63: "It is the spirit that gives life, while the flesh is of no avail."
- Psalm 82:6: "I have said, ye are Gods."

A concluding question to the quotations above would be:
"If man has ever been a God, why did he cease to be a God?"

So, it seems to be true that if one's heart is without sin, all requests will be fulfilled.

[1]**KJV**: King James Version of the Bible.

Closing remarks

Religion was meant to make us believe and not to reflect upon. It did not provide us with a clear way, a road map and tools to accomplish things.

But the time is over! The road map is drawn, and the tools are available to walk the path and to achieve the goal.

The quotations from the Bible may not make sense right now, but during the study, by stepping onto the path and by applying the learned tools, the words will come to prove themselves.

We must only open our eyes.

The time of lies and oppression has ended.

Get up and walk the path, the path to freedom!

So, even if we bear a grudge towards the things that have happened to us, or about what is going on in this world, remember, we are a part of it, it is our world!

No God will take hate away from any person. It is one's personal belief, and, in the end, the individual is the one who believes in something. It is just a thought!

About the author

I, Wolfgang Fries, was born in St. Wendel/ Saarland, Germany, on January 16, 1966. I had a standard education that included technical school. Afterward, I served five years in the Bundeswehr (German army) until 1994, when I started working as a stucco master, an occupation that enriched my life. I was easily able to form social contacts and was still well-liked after work. By forming a few friendships, I felt a social bond with others.

Unfortunately, I had to stop this nice work. As it turned out, bad things can lead to a good result. If I were not sitting in a wheelchair, I never would have written all of this. During a disastrous accident with the motorcycle, I broke my spine and since then have been permanently paralyzed.

But there is something in life everyone should know: Life itself. During all the work one does, and all the good times one enjoys, one should never forget this.

Exactly that was my endeavor.

It is not easy to find out what or who you are. If you're a tradesman, engineer, thinker, or racing professional ...

You can be anything, you only must decide!

Philosophie des Lebens - Das Buch der Grundlagen -

Was sind die Grundlagen des Daseins? Welche Geisteshaltung bedarf es in der heutigen Zeit um im Leben bestehen zu können, um Glück und Wohlergehen zu erfahren? Was ist wichtig zu wissen?

Der Mensch selbst, als denkendes Wesen ist der Ansicht, dass seine mächtigste Waffe der Verstand ist. Aufgrund seiner Fähigkeit zu denken hat er sich die Erde zum Untertan gemacht. Und tatsächlich, das Denken bestimmt das Handeln des Menschen, der Mensch ist nur so stabil wie sein Gedanke.

Der Gedanke selbst fußt auf Grundlagen die bestimmend dazu sind, wie man überlebt. So versucht der Mensch sich selbst, sein Denken und Handeln, die Welt um sich herum zu verstehen.

Verstehen: Was ist wichtiger als Verstehen selbst?

Grundlagen komprimiert verpackt, in kurzen Texten dargestellt. Mehr als 200 Essays führen den Leser zu mehr Verstehen im Leben und über das Leben selbst, sei es nun über den Menschen, das Denken, Glücklichsein, Beziehung, Lernen, Beruf, den Ursprung von Krankheiten, gesellschaftliches Dasein, Religion, Politik oder Freiheit.

Die Probleme des Menschen werden von der Ursache her geschildert und Lösungen angeboten. Es macht einen Unterschied dieses Wissen zu haben und sich dadurch selbst zu helfen.

„Philosophie des Lebens – Das Buch der Grundlagen" ist der Gesamt-Band welcher die Bücher „Meine Philosophie", „Lernen wie man lernt, lernen wie man versteht", „Eine glückliche Beziehung führen", „Rückführung – Einführung und Kurzanleitung" und ehemals „Im Leben bestehen – Die Bibel des 21sten Jahrhunderts" in einem Buch vereint.

Als Taschenbuch oder als Bibliotheken-Ausgabe im extra stabilen Hardcover-Format und Fadenbindung herausgegeben.

Philosophie des Lebens - Das Buch der Grundlagen -; 656 Seiten, 2017.

ISBN: **978-3-7357-8561-9** - Hardcover
ISBN: **978-3-7460-2923-8** - Taschenbuch